STEPHANIE LASHFORD

The Kitchen Crew

A Children's Wholefood Cookery Book

Illustrated in colour by
ADRIAN OBERTELLI

And in black and white by
FRASER MAY

ASHGROVE PRESS, BATH

14/-

mint.
from
Christmas
money.
Hal x x

As promised Jamie,
Good Cooking.
With love,
Sybil James
20. 7. 89.

Good Luck in SEPTEMBER.

First published in Great Britain by
ASHGROVE PRESS LIMITED
4 Brassmill Centre, Brassmill Lane
Bath BA1 3JN

Text © Stephanie Lashford 1989
Colour Illustrations © Adrian Obertelli 1989
Line Illustrations and Introduction © Ashgrove Press Ltd 1989

First published 1989

Lashford, Stephanie
The kitchen crew : a children's wholefood
cookery book.
1. cookery (Natural foods) — Juvenile literature
I. Title II. Obertelli, Adrian
641.5'637   TX652.5

ISBN 0 – 906798 – 63 – 9 Pbk

Photoset in Souvenir by
Ann Buchan (Typesetters) Middlesex
Printed in Great Britain
by Hillman Printers (Frome) Ltd

Dedicated to my godson
Ian Harvey
as requested

Acknowledgements

I would like to thank Mrs Anita Thomas and the Home
Economics Department of Cardiff High School for their
enthusiastic help in testing the recipes in this book. My
special thanks to the six who appear in the photograph on
the back cover. I would also like to thank C. Roberts for
taking the photograph.

The publishers would like to thank Tina Ryan for
The Body Bus.

Contents

The Body Bus

Roll up roll up!

All aboard for the great mystery tour, an incredible underground voyage of discovery, an adventure you will never forget.

Gasp as the coach guides you through the mighty cavernous *MOUTH*, then hold on to your hats as you hurtle down the breathtaking *GULLET*.

It's your chance in a lifetime to see for yourselves the *INTERNAL ORGANS* of the body. Bathe in those glorious *GASTRIC JUICES*! Take that magical twisting, turning journey through the *SMALL* and *LARGE INTESTINES*!

A few lucky trippers will visit the exciting *LIVER*, the fun-packed *KIDNEYS*, and frolic in the warm, inviting, *BLOODSTREAM*!

There are so many thrilling places to visit on this trip many of you will want to stay in the body forever. But for those of you who take the full journey, don't forget to visit the glorious, picturesque *RECTUM* before you leave. You'll be spellbound!

Who will be chosen to take this wonderful trip? There's only limited space on board.

You'll have to be rather special to qualify, you'll have to look good, smell good and taste good. The human body is particular, it doesn't take just anyone. The body has spies who will test all trippers before allowing them on board.

You have to get past the eyes and nose. And the tastebuds in the departure area, (known as the mouth). If you can pass these, you're on your way to a journey of a lifetime.

By now readers will have guessed the 'voyage' in question is the journey your food takes through your digestive system.

You'll know from school trips and holidays, that the success of any trip can depend on who's on the coach.

Trouble-makers, vandals and loud-mouths can spoil things for everyone.

But some people are really useful to have along. The coach driver, for instance, a guide, someone who can read a map. It might also be useful to take along someone who could repair the coach if it broke down.

It's even more important that we choose very carefully which foods we allow on board our bodies as each passenger has a vital job to do once inside the body.

Our brains, with the help of our eyes, noses, and tastebuds as 'spies', decide which foods can come on board.

Your Brain Speaking

"Hello, hello, this is your brain speaking. I want full reports, eyes, nose and tongue, full information about all the passengers attempting to board this bus.

This body doesn't want any trouble-makers inside. The truth is, there is a lot of work to be done on this monument, extensions are needed to the arms and legs, for instance. We'll need the materials for making new bones and muscle.

The outside could do with a fresh lick of paint, too, that means we need the right foods for making new skin, bright eyes and shining hair.

And just look at the state of those teeth! The last coach party included a couple of sticky buns and a jelly. What louts! They started attacking the teeth before they even got on board the bus!''

Your body's spies are doubtless alert. No plate of worms, rotten eggs or burnt custard would get past your eyes, nose and tastebuds.

But are you sure only useful passengers are getting on board?

Are any trouble-makers wheedling their way on to the bus? This book will help your spies to spot the trouble-makers in their tracks. They may try to sneak on board when you're not looking. They may arrive at the departure point in disguise.

So How Do You Spot A Wholefood?

A good guide is that a wholefood is one which appears on your plate very close to the way nature makes it.

Try this test. Which is the wholefood, the orange or the orange squash? Quite right, the orange. There it is on your plate, just the way it was when it was picked from the tree.

But the squash was produced in a factory with the help of all kinds of chemicals and machinery. The orange taste may come from a chemical, not a real orange at all. A bit of a cheat, really.

Which is the wholefood, the jacket potato or the packet of crisps? Right again, the potato, little changed since it was dug out of the ground. The crisps were made with potatoes, but much has been added. Take a look at the list of ingredients. There's a lot there that didn't grow in a field!

There are all kinds of wholefoods you have probably been enjoying for years without realising they were good for you.

Think of milk, apples, crunchy celery, yoghurt, the nuts you crack at Christmas time, the raisins you pinch on baking day, all excellent wholefoods.

When you eat natural foods, your body's spies know what's coming. A banana is a banana, plain and simple. But manufactured foods are not always what they seem.

Train your body's eye-spies to become label-spotters. They'll discover all sorts of strange things on labels. A meat or fruit pie might contain 'shaped pieces'. You may find the appetising pink of a raspberry mousse, or the golden breadcrumbs on your fish-fingers, are colours produced in a laboratory, and the delicious strawberry flavour of that lolly came from a test-tube, not a strawberry field.

You'll soon have your own black-list of phrases which mean your eyes and tastebuds are being deceived.

With a little thought you can reduce the number of manufactured foods you eat and replace them with natural ones, and still include plenty of your favourites in your new, healthy diet.

Natural, unsweetened orange juice is far more refreshing than a sugary, fizzy drink. Ever tried cheese and raw onion? That will fill you up better than a packet of cheese and onion crisps. A raw carrot makes a tasty snack.

Not everything that comes from a factory is loaded with cheats and liars. Many manufacturers these days are realising that people want real food, not a chemical cocktail. Look out for labels that say 'natural', 'additive-free', 'no artificial colours or flavours'.

Your eye-spies will tell you that some brands of peanut butter, for example, contain just roasted peanuts and sea salt.

Most bread (particularly the sort that's not swathed in polythene) is pure and wholesome. And what can be nicer than chunks torn off a newly-baked loaf, still warm from the oven, nibbled on the way home from the shops? Isn't that nicer than a gob-stopper?

We haven't yet answered the important question:

The Food, The Whole Food and Nothing But The Food

And that's where wholefood spotting comes in. An easy way to make sure that the foods that board your body bus are the right ones, is to choose a good variety of wholefoods, and avoid manufactured and processed foods.

This may seem complicated but when you have read this book you will know a lot more about what happens to food in your body, which foods help which bits of you to work well, and how to spot the 'goodies' from the 'baddies'.

No-one's asking you to cut out the 'baddies' altogether. But once you've tried some of the recipies which start on page . . . you may never want to eat junk food again!

Who Wants To Eat Wholefood Anyway?

Research shows that a lot of the illnesses suffered by people in quite well-off countries like ours, are probably due to the kind of food we eat.

Scientists have studied the kind of diet we eat now, and compared it with the kind of diet we used to eat in this country 200 years ago, when we ate more naturally. They have also looked at the diet of people who still live in primitive societies where there are no sweet shops, chip shops and burger bars.

And they think we should go back to eating the way we used to eat if we want to stay healthy. We should eat a lot less sugar and salt, for instance, and less fat, and a lot more fibre.

Eating a banana instead of a bag of sweets won't make you feel instantly healthy, of course. But eating a lot of unhealthy food over a long period may cause problems in the future.

You may think that illnesses that happen to adults are not very important to you now. You have to die of something in the end, why not enjoy yourself while you're here?

Very logical. But remember there are unpleasant things that happen to young people because of the food they eat. Spotty skin, excess flab, greasy hair and bad teeth are not a lot of fun.

What Is Food?

We all need food, everyone knows that. We need food to grow, to give us energy, to swim a hundred yards or play a game of football, to keep warm, to fight off disease, to help our bodies to heal when we are injured.

To do all this we need a mixture of several different kinds of food. That is what is meant by 'a balanced meal' or 'a balanced diet'.

Getting the right mix of passengers on the body bus is the way to a healthy future. So don't let just anyone on your body bus.

Proteins — The Building Construction and Repair Squad

The proteins you eat go to work building all that new bone and flesh to make you inches taller by your next birthday. And if you are unlucky enough to break a bone or cut yourself, those helpful protein chaps will get right down to building replacement bone and tissue.

Protein is found in meat, fish, eggs, milk, cheese, peas, beans, lentils, nuts and cereals. In fact, almost all the basic foods contain some protein.

It's an important part of the plan to let proteins on the bus at every mealtime. Young people who are still growing need more than adults who only need protein for running repairs.

It is sensible to eat proteins from different sources. It makes good sense, for example, to eat chilli beans with minced beef — this gives you a mixture of different proteins. So do beans on toast, cereal with milk, and pasta and beans.

Carbohydrates For Energy

Carbohydrates are big and friendly, cheap and cheerful. They'll make the coach party go with a swing because they always have bags of energy.

We usually get ours from foods like bread, potatoes and rice.

They also give us that lovely full, satisfied feeling. They'll take up lots of room on the bus, but with carbohydrates spreading themselves on three seats at a time, there's less room on board for vandals and troublemakers — and we know who they are, don't we? Yes, sugar, cakes, greasy crisps and chips.

Eat a good wholesome sandwich with a protein filling for lunch, and you're less likely to be tempted by sweets, that's the message.

Carbohydrates are more than just filling. Without them our bodies would use up those valuable proteins for instant energy, instead of allowing them to get on with their important body-building work.

You wouldn't use your tennis racket or violin for fire-wood. That would be a waste of a valuable piece of equipment. Much better to burn something that's more suited to the job and is no use for anything else.

Proteins are your body's violins, and cheap, filling carbohydrates are the firewood. Whoever buys the food in your home will gladly tell you it's cheaper to fill up on wholemeal bread than steak.

But remember your body needs both. So eating meat with potatoes, or a peanut butter sandwich, is very well balanced.

Vitamins And Minerals

If you could see a vitamin or mineral, in the sort of quantities taken in at a meal, they would look pretty small and insignificant. But they all have very important jobs to do.

While the big chaps like protein and carbohydrate can turn their hands to a variety of tasks, vitamins, minerals (and some even smaller friends, trace elements), all have very specific, and very important jobs to do.

No member of this family can do the job of any other. But they often work in teams. For example vitamins A and

D team up with protein and a couple of minerals in the teeth and bone production department. They often travel together, too. They are all found in eggs and milk. A and D and calcium are found together in butter and cod liver oil, and A is also found in apricots.

Calcium is also found in flour, bread, oatmeal, nuts, sesame seeds, soybeans, turnips and greens.

We can also eat calcium by eating the bones of other creatures — like the soft bones in sardines and tinned salmon.

Calcium also does other skilled work such as helping muscles to form properly, and helping the blood to clot when we cut ourselves.

Then there's the vitamin B gang — there are several of those, and their job includes the production of red blood cells. The B family are found in meat, beans, yeasty foods, whole grains, raw carrots and cabbage.

Vitamin C, found in citrus fruits like oranges and lemons, also tomatoes, brussel sprouts and peppers, stop us from getting a disease called scurvy, which used to afflict sailors on long voyages when they could not get hold of fresh fruit.

The other member of this family you've probably heard of is iron. Iron also works hard on the formation of red blood cells, and in the muscle and energy departments. Iron needs a partner too. The more vitamin C you eat the more of the iron can be absorbed. So eat plenty of fresh veg with your meat next Sunday!

Iron is found in liver, kidneys, egg yolk, almonds, raisins, meat, shellfish, molasses, potatoes, cabbage, even in plain water.

It would be exhausting to try to plan every meal to contain all the vitamins and minerals you need in a day. The best plan is to eat a variety including as many fresh and unprocessed foods as you can. And do try to eat raw fruit and vegetables sometimes, as cooking can destroy most of these vital little travellers.

This way you can be fairly confident your vitamin, mineral and trace element intake are sufficient.

Fibre — The Driving Force

Fibre, who also has another name, roughage, is a jolly useful person to have on the bus. Without fibre, everything we eat would move so slowly that our digestive systems would be overloaded.

Fibre is the structural parts of fruit, vegetables and nuts — the cell walls. The peel on a potato, the skin on an apple, are both very visible forms of fibre. You can also actually see the cell walls of an orange, they're all those chewy bits that stop the orange juice from falling out.

The fibrous part of the plant has no nutritional value on its own, but our digestive systems like it better when they have to gnaw through nature's own 'packaging' to get at the goodies within.

Fibre also acts as a natural rationing system. Just imagine if every individual toffee in the world was wrapped in silver paper, then cellophane, then put in a box and tied up with string. You wouldn't be able to eat very many during school break-time.

Natural foods with plenty of fibre, like fresh fruit and raw vegetables also have lots of 'packaging' and the time it takes us to munch through it all, means we can't eat too much, and we don't get fat. You can see how easy it is to get fat on foods like chocolate or jelly, when the manufacturer has done all the work for you.

Once inside the body, fibre helps to keep the food

moving through the passages that form the digestive tract. Our bodies without fibre are like a bus without a driver.

Sugar — The False Friend

Oh no, here comes the first trouble-maker, trying to hitch a ride on the bus. Sugar is one passenger you can do without. You may have heard people say that everyone needs sugar for energy. They are not telling you the whole truth. All foods are capable of providing energy, and we have just seen that a potato or a slice of bread are excellent energy foods.

Sugar can provide energy, but really it's a false friend. Refined sugar, that's the kind in the sugar bowl, comes from two plants called sugar beet and sugar cane. If you were to munch on the raw plant, several things would happen. You'd enjoy the sweet taste, but you'd also be eating vitamins, minerals and fibre, all useful to the body. And you'd be pretty full by the time you had chewed enough to swallow a teaspoon of sugar as we know it. And your jaws, teeth and gums would have had some healthy exercise, too.

If you suck a sugar cube, what happens? You know the sugar would do ghastly things to your teeth. It would also slip down your throat very quickly, leaving you just as hungry as before. And because the refining process which extracted the sweet, white substance from the plant also removed most of the vitamins and minerals and all the fibre, the sugar hasn't done your body any favours at all.

And as you still feel hungry you are likely to eat more food. By eating food where the manufacturer has done all the work for you, you need more to fill you up. And when you eat more than your body needs what happens? The extra is stored as fat. To avoid this eat more natural, unprocessed foods.

If nature has given you a sweet tooth, you can satisfy it by using the naturally sweet foods that nature has provided, like fresh fruit, raisins, currants, and dates.

Instead of sprinkling sugar on your breakfast cereal, try adding a handful of raisins or sultanas to your cereal, and you'll be getting fibre, minerals and vitamins as well as a sweet taste.

There's even natural sugar in onions, beetroot, parsnips and carrots. Have you ever tried carrot cake? It's delicious, and carrots are highly nutritious, a much better deal than that false friend, refined sugar.

Fats

We need some fat for energy and to keep us warm, but most of us in modern well-off countries eat far too much fat. We know we are eating fat when we have butter on our bread, or cream on our pudding. Cheese is also a form of fat, but as it contains many other nutrients such as calcium, protein and vitamins, cheese is not altogether a 'baddy', especially cottage cheese, Fromage Frais and the new low-fat hard cheeses that taste just as good as Cheddar.

But fats often sneak on board the body bus as the 'excess baggage' of other foods. Crisps and chips bring on board masses of fat we can well do without. Doctors and scientists are seriously worried that the quantities of these foods that most children like to eat will store up serious health problems for the future.

Fat also lurks in chocolate, biscuits, cakes and pastry. You wouldn't dream of spooning down a tub of lard, but by eating all these foods that's just what you are doing.

You may ask what's wrong with fat? Well, for a start, excess fat makes you fat. There is a great deal of potential energy contained in fat. An ounce of butter contains far more energy than an ounce of chocolate, and as much as four times as much energy as a slice of bread. It's a very concentrated food, so it's easy to eat more than the body can use up in a day. And the body stores the excess as fat. The fatter you become, the less you feel like running about and burning it off, and so you sit on the sidelines, munch another packet of crisps, and grow even unhappier. Ugh!

In addition, large quantities of animal fat can really gum up the works, causing blockages in your arteries, for example, which may lead to heart disease.

And don't forget fat, along with that false friend sugar, causes spots and pimples too.

Fat and sugar are generally not nice. But although we can do without refined sugar, we do need some fat on board, and vegetable fats are our best allies. Again, stick to natural foods, where fat occurs in naturally regulated amounts, and cut down on manufactured foods where fat is added artificially.

You can soon get used to bread, potatoes and greens without lashings of butter or margarine, but if you do like to gild the lily, choose margarines that are rich in polyunsaturates, and do your body a favour.

Additives — Cheats And Loudmouths

There's a group of gate-crashers who appear more and more often these days whenever a coach is about to take the great underground body journey. They are called Chemical Additives, and quite frankly, they're a bunch of show-offs who try to pretend they're something they're not.

They are artificial substances which make manufactured foods look, smell and taste delicious, and last a long time on the supermarket shelf. But they cheat your eyes, nose and tastebuds.

Chemicals can be used in the manufacture of foods to do all kinds of things: to make a lolly taste orangey, to make a yoghurt look pink and raspberry-ish, to give the pastry on a pie an appetising sheen, to keep an old sausage from going bad in the supermarket fridge, to glue together the ingredients of, say, peanut butter so that they don't separate when the jar is left to stand in the larder.

But really, wouldn't you rather enjoy the taste of a real orange or raspberry, eat a freshly-baked pie, forget the fatty sausage altogether, and if the peanut butter separates a little in the jar, it's not much trouble to stir it up a little before spreading it on the bread!

But are additives necessarily bad for you?

All additives have to be rigorously tested before they can be used on food. Nevertheless, additives have been blamed for a number of ills, such as headaches and allergies.

As yet we do not know what are the long-term effects of a daily diet of manufactured breakfast cereal, a bought burger, choc bar and a can of fizzy drink, followed by a supper of a bought pie with tinned vegetables and a mousse from the freezer. You'd be eating a real cocktail of additives there, and no-one knows what the effect might be in future years.

So yet again follow the advice from the guys on the coach — you are what you eat, so eat naturally.

The Body Bus begins its journey on page 33.

Spicy Vegetable Samosas

You will need

INGREDIENTS

Pastry
350 g (12 oz) self raising wholemeal flour
175 g (6 oz) polyunsaturated margarine
Cold water

Filling
2 carrots, washed and diced very small
(the size of a frozen pea)
1 parsnip, washed and diced very small
4 medium potatoes, diced very small
4 tablesp. Frozen Peas
1 heaped teasp. curry powder

EQUIPMENT

saucepan & lid   grater
mixing bowl   round-ended knife
rolling pin   greased baking tray
sharp knife   ruler

WHAT TO DO

1   Place all the filling ingredients into the saucepan, cover with 150 ml (¼ pt) cold
    water and simmer until tender. Put to one side to cool.
    Micro-Tip: place in microwave with 30 ml (2 tablesps.) cold water, cook for 5–7
    minutes until tender, at full power.

2   Pre-heat the oven to 200C, 400°F, Gas Mark 6. Prepare the pastry. Place the flour
    in the mixing bowl and rub in the margarine until it resembles breadcrumbs. Add
    enough cold water to give a firm, soft dough.

3   Knead gently on the table top and divide into 4 equal pieces. Roll each piece into a
    15 cm (6″) square. Place ¼ of the filling into the centre of a square. Wet one edge
    and fold to give a triangle. Using a sharp knife, cut in half and press edges together
    to seal. Repeat with the remaining pastry squares.

4   Bake for 20–25 minutes until well risen.

Serve hot with natural yoghurt, flavoured with freshly chopped mint for a special
supper.

Cheese and Sweetcorn Quiche

You will need

INGREDIENTS

Pastry
130 g (5 oz) plain wholemeal flour
25 g (1 oz) cornflour
25 g (1 oz) polyunsaturated margarine
25 g (1 oz) vegetable margarine
very cold water

Filling
2 eggs, size 3, well beaten
100 g (4 oz) edam or reduced fat cheddar cheese, grated
60 ml (4 heaped tablesps.) sweetcorn
45 ml (3 tablesps.) milk

EQUIPMENT

mixing bowl
round-ended knife
rolling pin

20 cm (8″) flan dish
small bowl
fork

WHAT TO DO

1   Mix flour and cornflour together in a large mixing bowl.
2   Cut the margarine into pieces the size of your little fingernail and add to the flour.
3   Using your fingertips rub the fat into the flour, until it resembles breadcrumbs.
4   Slowly add 10 ml (2 teaspoons) of very cold water to every 25 g (1 oz) flour. Using a rounded knife mix until a soft dough is formed.
5   Place on a floured surface and knead gently until you have a smooth dough.
6   Roll out until the pastry is the correct size for the dish.
7   Line the flan dish and leave in fridge.
8   Pre-heat the oven to 190C, 375°F, Gas Mark 5.
9   *Prepare the filling*: beat the eggs well, add the grated cheese and sweetcorn.
10 Pour into the pastry base, place flan dish on a baking tray and bake for 35 minutes or until firm.

To serve: arrange tomato and mustard and cress neatly around the edge.
Can be eaten hot or cold.

Pitta Sandwiches

Use pitta bread — an unleavened bread from Greece — to make a sandwich-in-a-pocket.

You will need

INGREDIENTS

wholemeal pitta bread
filling (*see recipes below*)

EQUIPMENT

bread board
bread knife
metal spoon
toaster (or use the grill, or oven on low setting)

WHAT TO DO

1 Cut the pitta bread in half and warm in toaster, grill or oven.
2 Open the warmed bread to make a pocket and spoon in your favourite filling. Try the ideas below, or invent your own.

Filling (1): Luigi's vegetable spaghetti mixture (see p. 23)

Filling (2): Coleslaw and warm baked beans

Filling (3): Cottage cheese, baked beans and salad

Filling (4): Cold rice pudding and chopped apple

Pinwheel Savoury

You will need

INGREDIENTS

3 large potatoes for the base
milk and margarine to mix
100 g (4 oz) grated cheese
3 tomatoes, sliced
60 ml (4 tablesp.) sweetcorn
pepper, washed and diced
1 very small can baked beans

EQUIPMENT

potato peeler
tin opener
medium saucepan with well-fitting lid
potato masher
cheese grater
sharp vegetable knife
chopping board
13–15 cm (7–8″) heat-proof dinner plate
fork

WHAT TO DO

1 Pre-heat oven to 170C, 325°F, Gas Mark 3.
2 Thinly peel the potatoes and place in the saucepan. Cover with water and put on the lid. Heat until boiling.
3 Reduce the heat and simmer for 20 mins or until they are soft all the way through.
4 Drain the water off and mash with the margarine, then using a fork beat in the milk.
5 Spread the mashed potato to make a circle over a heat-proof plate.
6 Use the beans to make a centre to the wheel, and then make concentric circles using the pepper, sweetcorn, tomatoes and cheese.
7 *To serve*: place in the oven for 15 minutes or microwave on high for 2 minutes.

Makes 2–3 portions

Superspuds

You will need

INGREDIENTS

2 large potatoes weighing up to
225 g (8 oz)

EQUIPMENT

kitchen towel
baking tray
fork

WHAT TO DO

1   Pre-heat the oven to 190C, 375°F, Gas Mark 5.
2   Scrub the potatoes very well using a kitchen brush.
3   Dry with the kitchen towel.
4   Using a fork, prick the potato several times. Pop onto a baking tray.
5   Put in the oven and leave to cook for 1½ hours. Test to see if cooked by prodding with a fork to see if the inside is soft. If not, leave for a further 15 minutes.

HOW TO MAKE YOUR BAKED POTATOES INTO "SUPER SPUDS"

1   Scoop out the middle and mix the soft potato with one of the following:
    Baked beans;
    30 ml (2 tablesps.) of natural yoghurt and 50 g (2 oz) peanuts;
    50 g (2 oz) grated cheese;
    15 ml (1 tablesp.) of tomato ketchup and some chopped pickled onion.
    Put the filling back in and reheat for a further 15 minutes.
2   Alternatively, using a fork, push the cooked potato aside until you have made a well. Then drop an egg into the well, rebake until the egg is cooked. This is very filling and can be eaten as a snack.

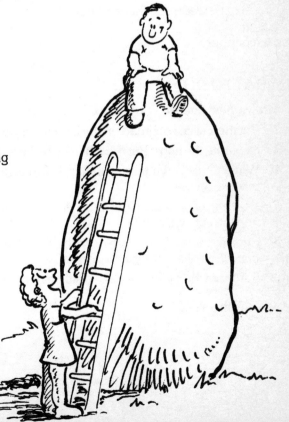

Toasted Cheese Soufflé

You will need

INGREDIENTS

2 slices wholemeal bread
3 eggs, size 3/4
75 g (3 oz) fat reduced cheese, finely grated
dash pepper

EQUIPMENT

baking tray   hand whisk
egg separator   fork
plate   metal spoon
grater   2 bowls, 1 large, 1 small

WHAT TO DO

1 Pre-heat oven to 200C, 400°F, Gas Mark 6.
2 Put the 2 slices of bread on the baking tray and place in the oven for 8–10 mins.
3 Separate the eggs. Put the white in the large bowl and the yolk in the small.
4 Whisk until the whites are firm and you can turn the bowl upside down without the mixture moving.
5 Beat egg yolks with a fork and, using the metal spoon, fold the yolks and cheese into the egg white.
6 Remove bread from oven, turn the slices over and spoon the soufflé mixture on to them. Sprinkle lightly with pepper.
7 Return to the oven and bake until golden brown, for 6–10 minutes.

Serve with a salad.

   Makes a snack lunch for 2

French Toast

Tout les posh recipe books sont full of French recipes, so ici un recipe Français supérieur from the Kitchen Crew. Ooh, là, là!

You will need

INGREDIENTS

15 ml (1 tablesp.) skimmed milk
2 eggs
pinch ground black pepper
2 thick slices wholemeal bread
15 ml (1 tablesp.) vegetable oil

EQUIPMENT

small mixing bowl
spatula
non-stick frying pan
warmed serving plates
fork

METHOD

1 Break the eggs into the mixing bowl, add the milk and a pinch of pepper and beat well with the fork.
2 Heat the oil gently in the frying pan.
3 Dip the bread in the egg mixture, then carefully place the eggy bread in the frying pan.
4 After about two minutes, use the spatula to carefully lift one corner of the bread to see if it has gone brown, which means that it's ready. When it is, turn it and cook the other side for about the same length of time.
5 Serve straight away on warmed plates.

Delicious with grilled tomatoes or sprinkled with grated cheese.

Makes 2 portions

Vegetable Tortillas

You will need

INGREDIENTS

1 small onion, chopped
15 ml (1 tablesp.) vegetable oil
3 ml (½ teasp.) chilli powder
3 ml (½ teasp.) ground cumin
1 clove garlic, crushed (optional)
30 ml (2 tablesps.) tomato purée
150 ml (¼ pt) water

1 small green pepper, diced
1 small red pepper, diced
60 ml (4 tablesps.) sweetcorn
1 small tin red kidney beans
100 g (4 oz) grated cheddar cheese
6 ready prepared taco shells

EQUIPMENT

saucepan
sharp knife
chopping board
grater

wooden spoon
measuring jug
metal spoon
serving plate

WHAT TO DO

1 Heat the oil and gently fry the onion for 2 minutes over a low heat. Add the chilli powder, ground cumin, and garlic (if used), and gently fry for a further 2 minutes. Add diced peppers and cook for another 2 minutes.

2 Add the tomato purée and water, stir well and cook for 10 minutes.

3 Pre-heat the oven to 170C, 325°F, Gas Mark 3.

4 Add the kidney beans and sweetcorn. Continue cooking slowly for 10 minutes.

5 Fill the taco shells with the vegetable mixture and top with the grated cheese. Heat through in the oven for 5–10 minutes per 6 taco shells.
Micro-tip: heat each taco shell through for 1 minute on a low temperature.

6 *To serve*: eat on their own or with shredded lettuce or coleslaw.

American Coleslaw

Coleslaw is a very versatile dish and variations to the basic recipe are almost endless.
Here is one for you to try.

You will need

INGREDIENTS

¼ white cabbage, washed
2 carrots, peeled
1 small onion, peeled
1 large crispy apple
1 x 150 ml (5 fl. oz) carton natural yoghurt
10 ml (2 teasps.) salad cream

EQUIPMENT

sharp knife
chopping board
large mixing bowl
small mixing bowl
grater
tablespoon

WHAT TO DO

1 Finely slice the cabbage. Place in a large mixing bowl.
2 Carefully grate the apple, onion and carrots, making sure not to grate your own fingers. Add to the bowl.
3 Mix together the yoghurt and salad cream.
4 Using a tablespoon, stir yoghurt mixture into vegetables, mixing well.

For a change, why not vary the ingredients? Try peanuts, walnuts, sweetcorn, grapes, orange segments, pineapple chunks, raisins and sultanas, sunflower seeds, and sesame seeds.

Mexican Hat Salad

Don't try to go to sleep under this tasty salad. Try it as a packed lunch instead.

You will need

INGREDIENTS

1 lettuce, finely shredded
½ onion, sliced into rings
2 tomatoes, diced
1 ripe avocado, skinned and sliced
1 small tin red kidney beans, drained

6 sprigs parsley or coriander, chopped
1 small tin tuna in brine, flaked
juice of 1 lemon
½ packet tortilla chips

EQUIPMENT

chopping board
fork
mixing spoon
sharp knife

lemon squeezer
serving bowl
tin opener
mixing bowl

WHAT TO DO

1   At least half an hour before you want to eat, mix together all the ingredients except the tortilla chips.

2   *To serve*: arrange in a serving bowl with the tortilla chips around the edge.

This is a salad that's a meal in itself.

Luigi's Vegetable Spaghetti

You will need

INGREDIENTS

100 g (4 oz) mushrooms, sliced
1 medium aubergine, diced
2 tomatoes, sliced
1 onion, sliced
1 clove garlic
1 red pepper, washed, deseeded & diced
1 green pepper, washed, deseeded & diced

150 ml (¼ pt) water
30 ml (2 tablesps.) vegetable oil
good pinch oregano
15 ml (1 heaped tablesp.) Pesto (optional)
at least 50 g (2 oz) uncooked spaghetti per person
50 g (2 oz) strong cheddar cheese, grated

EQUIPMENT

2 large saucepans with lids
wooden spoon
chopping board
sharp knife
tablespoon
grater
warmed serving bowl

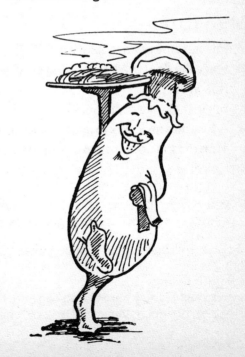

WHAT TO DO

1   Heat 15 ml (1 tablesp.) oil in a large saucepan, add the onions, garlic, and aubergine, and cook for 2 minutes.

2   Add the peppers, mushrooms, tomatoes and oregano. Continue to cook for a further 2 minutes. Add the water, cover, and simmer until the vegetables are tender – for about 10 minutes.

3   Fill the second large saucepan with cold water, add to this the second 15 ml (1 tablesp.) of oil. Bring to the boil and add the spaghetti. Stir once to ensure the spaghetti does not stick. Cook until tender – for approximately 20 minutes.

To serve: drain the spaghetti and place in the serving bowl. Stir in the Pesto. Pour over the vegetable sauce and sprinkle on the grated cheese.

This dish is rich in fibre, vitamins and minerals, and should be included in a healthy diet. It is also low in cholesterol and salt.

Makes 9 portions

Stepping Stones Scones

You will need

INGREDIENTS

225 g (8 oz) fine milled self-raising
wholemeal flour
50 g (2 oz) polyunsaturated margarine
25 g (1 oz) raw cane sugar or 25 g (1 oz)
sultanas (leave out for savoury varieties)
150 ml (¼ pt) skimmed milk

EQUIPMENT

large mixing bowl
measuring jug
round-ended knife
baking tray
5 cm (2") cutter
pastry brush

WHAT TO DO

1   Pre-heat the oven to 220C, 425°F, Gas Mark 7.
2   Place the flour in a large mixing bowl.
3   Rub in the fat.
4   Stir in the sugar or sultanas.
5   Add all the milk. Mix to a soft dough using a round-ended knife.
6   Turn out the dough on to a floured surface, and knead gently until smooth.
7   Roll out to 1 cm (½") thickness and cut out the scones using a 5 cm (2") cutter. Place on a greased baking tray.
8   Brush with a little milk and place on the top shelf of the oven and cook for 12–15 minutes. until well risen and golden brown.

To serve: split and spread with polyunsaturated margarine or the spread of your choice.
Suggested fillings:
egg and parsley — 1 hard boiled egg and 3 sprigs of parsley finely chopped;
25 g (1 oz) peanut butter and 50 g (2 oz) cheese; grated apple and cinnamon.

Wholemeal Welsh Cakes

You will need

INGREDIENTS

175 g (6 oz) fine milled wholemeal self
raising flour
50 g (2 oz) polyunsaturated margarine
50 g (2 oz) raw cane sugar eg Golden
Granulated sugar

50 g (2 oz) currants
1 egg, size 3
2 tablesps. milk
pinch mixed spice or ground mace

EQUIPMENT

mixing bowl
round-ended knife
rolling pin
2" cutter
griddle (or heavy frying pan)

palette knife
cooling rack
metal spoon
small bowl

WHAT TO DO

1 Place the flour into a large mixing bowl and rub in the fat.

2 Stir in the sugar, currants and mixed spice using a metal spoon.

3 Beat the egg and milk together in small bowl using a fork.

4 Mix into the dry ingredients until you have a soft dough.

5 Knead gently on a floured table top and roll out until 6 mm (¼") thick.

6 Cut using a 5 cm (2") cutter.

7 Cook on a greased griddle or use a heavy frying pan allowing 5 minutes each side,
turning once with the palette knife.

Makes 24

Fruity Jack

You will need

INGREDIENTS

200 g (7 oz) rolled oats
100 g (4 oz) vegetable margarine
225 g (8 oz) syrup or maple syrup
100 g (4 oz) raw cane sugar eg Golden
Granulated sugar
50 g (2 oz) chopped raisins

EQUIPMENT

medium saucepan
wooden spoon
cooling rack
chopping knife
chopping board
tablespoon

WHAT TO DO

1 Pre-heat oven to 180C, 350°F, Gas Mark 4.
2 Melt the vegetable margarine, syrup and raw cane sugar in a medium sized saucepan. Do not allow to boil.
3 Add the chopped raisins.
4 Stir in the oats.
5 Grease a shallow tin about 25 cm x 15 cm (10 x 6″) and press the mixture into the tin, to a thickness of 6 mm (¼″).
6 Bake for 30 minutes until firm but not brown.
7 Cut into squares whilst still warm and remove when cool.

Excellent for packed meals and picnics. Rather sweet, so not something you should eat too much of!

Muesli Bars

You will need

INGREDIENTS

50 g (2 oz) apricots
50 g (2 oz) dates
50 g (2 oz) figs
50 g (2 oz) sultanas
50 g (2 oz) sunflower seeds

50 g (2 oz) hazelnuts
110 g (4 oz) medium porridge oats
15–30 ml (1–2 tablesps.) concentrated apple juice

EQUIPMENT

mixing bowl
chopping board
sharp knife
tablespoon
baking tin
large metal spoon

WHAT TO DO

1. Pre-heat oven to 180C, 350°F, Gas Mark 4.
2. Finely chop or mince the fruit and nuts, and mix thoroughly with the other ingredients.
3. Press into a lightly greased 18 cm (7'') square tin
4. Bake for 15 minutes. Cut into slices while still warm.

Intergalactic Moonrocks

You will need

INGREDIENTS

200 g (8 oz) self-raising wholemeal flour.
75 g (3 oz) polyunsaturated margarine.
75 g (3 oz) raw cane sugar
1 egg
skimmed milk to mix
100 g (4 oz) currants

EQUIPMENT

mixing bowl
metal spoon
round-ended knife
fork
greased baking tray
measuring jug

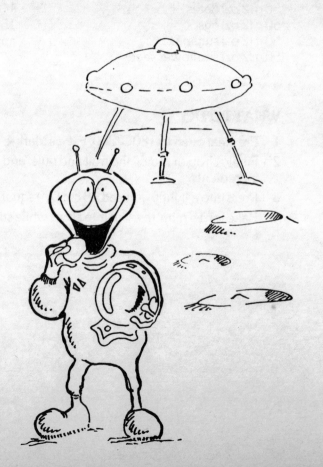

WHAT TO DO

1 Pre-heat the oven to 200C, 400°F, Gas Mark 6.
2 Place the flour in a mixing bowl and rub in the margarine.
3 Stir in the sugar and currants.
4 Beat the egg in the measuring jug and top up with milk to make 150 ml (¼ pt).
5 Add the milk mixture to the dry ingredients and mix to a soft dough using a knife.
6 Then, using a fork and spoon, place 12 equal amounts on the baking tray — they should have a roughness about them to look like rocks.
7 Bake for 15–20 minutes until well risen and golden brown.

Best eaten the same day, best of all still warm from the oven.

Sandwiches

Sandwiches are named after Lord Sandwich who, far too busy at his exciting card game to stop for lunch, sent his servant to fetch some food. When this arrived Lord Sandwich put it between two slices of bread and carried on playing while he ate. His invention was soon much imitated.

A sandwich can be as nutritious as a cooked meal, especially if you have a raw food filling. The best bread is wholemeal, containing the whole of the wheat grain and providing fibre, protein, carbohydrates and a variety of minerals (eg calcium). Nothing has been added or taken away, unlike white flour which has been bleached and contains additives. For a change try wholegrain rye bread. Also choose wholegrain crispbread (rye or wheat).

A healthy diet should be low in fats, especially animal fats. Vegetable fats, rich in polyunsaturates, are preferable, so look for margarines high in these. Low fat spreads are also valuable. Use butter sparingly. Some fillings taste even better without any spread at all.

SUGGESTED FILLINGS

1. Tuna and Mayonnaise with shredded lettuce
2. Grated cheese and pickle
3. Coleslaw and dill pickle
4. Vegetable paté and curly endive
5. Humus and cress
6. soaked bulgar wheat and fresh mint
7. Feta cheese and chopped black olives
8. Peanut butter and garam masala
9. Tahina and diced pepper
10. Almond butter and raisins
11. Fried Okra and curry powder, mashed
12. Grated carrot and lemon juice
13. Miso and shredded lettuce
14. Sweetcorn and apple in mayonnaise
15. Diced beetroot and natural yoghurt
16. Sugar free jam and thick set natural yoghurt
17. Cooked mincemeat and natural yoghurt
18. Crunchy peanut butter and mustard and cress
19. Lemon curd and chopped almonds
20. Mashed banana and cinnamon
21. Mashed banana, raisins and honey
22. Cottage cheese with pineapple
23. Cottage cheese with peaches
24. Cottage cheese with strawberries
25. Cottage cheese with raspberries
26. Cottage cheese with celery and chives
27. Chopped egg and parsley with mayonnaise
28. Honey and slices of apple
29. Mashed strawberries and honey
30. Hazelnut butter and carob bits
31. Shredded watercress and orange
32. Mashed avocado pear, lemon juice and black pepper
33. Avocado pears mashed in Thousand Island dressing
34. Grated cheese and sliced apple
35. Cheese and mayonnaise
36. Cheese and celery
37. Mashed banana and sliced apple
38. Vege burgers and mustard – grilled
39. Lettuce and grilled mushroom
40. Double decker salad sandwich: lettuce, tomato, cucumber, radish, spring onion, watercress
41. Mashed avocado pear and cottage cheese
42. Diced pineapple and grated carrot
43. Mayonnaise, peaches and raspberries
44. Grated carrots, raisins and mayonnaise
45. Cucumber, lettuce and mayonnaise
46. Honey, blackberries and sliced apple
47. Sliced tomato and onion with fresh mint
48. Cooked lentils and mayonnaise with fresh dill
49. Fromage Frais and chopped nuts
50. Raw young spinach leaves with mango chutney

The Gingerbread Family

You will need

INGREDIENTS

45 ml (3 tablesps.) soya oil
75 g (3 oz) raw cane sugar
75 g (3 oz) molasses
100 g (4 oz) wholemeal flour

100 g (4 oz) brown rice flour
10 ml (2 level teasps.) ground ginger
5 ml (1 level teasp.) bicarbonate of soda
currants for eyes and coat buttons

EQUIPMENT

saucepan
wooden spoon
rolling pin
mixing bowl
teaspoon

1–2 baking trays
flour dredger
paper, pencil
and scissors
sharp knife

Before you make the mixture take 3 sheets of paper and draw a mummy bear, a daddy bear and the bear children.

METHOD

1   Pre-heat the oven to 170C, 325°F, Gas Mark 3.

2   Put the oil and molasses in a saucepan and heat gently.

3   In a mixing bowl sieve all the dry ingredients together. Mix the bran back in if it separates out during sieving.

4   Pour the oil mix into the dry ingredients and mix well. Allow to cool slightly.

5   Roll out on a floured surface and cut using your bear shapes. Use the currants for eyes and buttons.

6   Bake for 10–15 mins. depending on size — keep well apart as they do spread. Leave on the tray to cool so that you don't break a leg or an arm.

Jam In The Hole Buns

You will need

INGREDIENTS

200 g (8 oz) self-raising wholemeal flour
50 g (2 oz) polyunsaturated margarine
50 g (2 oz) raw cane sugar
150 ml (¼ pt) skimmed milk
60 ml (4 tablesps.) sugar free raspberry
jam

EQUIPMENT

mixing bowl
metal spoon
round-ended knife
greased baking tray
teaspoon
wire rack

METHOD

1 Pre-heat oven to 200C, 400°F, Gas Mark 6.
2 Place the flour into a large mixing bowl.
3 Rub in the margarine until it resembles fine breadcrumbs and stir in the sugar.
4 Add the liquid slowly and mix to a firm dough using a round-ended knife.
5 Knead gently until the mixture is smooth.
6 Divide into 8 equal sized balls, and place on a greased baking tray.
7 Using a floured finger make little holes in the centre of each bun and fill with raspberry jam.
8 Bake in the middle or top of the oven for 15–20 minutes until well risen. Cool on a wire rack.

Eat the same day as they do not keep too well.

Unidentified Flying Pizza
Teatime Apple and Banana Pizza

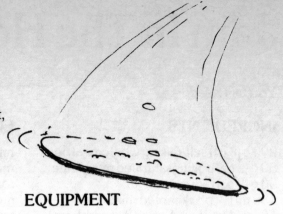

Do flying saucers really exist? Some people say that they have seen them in the sky, others that they have been taken aboard by strange-looking aliens. But if they do exist, what do they look like? Could they be flat, round and yellow. . . ?

You will need

INGREDIENTS

Base
250 g (8 oz) self raising wholemeal flour
50 g (2 oz) polyunsaturated margarine
50 g (2 oz) raw cane sugar
150 ml (¼ pt) natural yoghurt

Topping
1 banana, sliced
2 medium cooking apples, stewed and sweetened to taste
50 g (2 oz) plump dark raisins

EQUIPMENT

mixing bowl
scales
metal spoon
sharp knife

saucepan
round-ended knife
rolling pin
greased baking tray

Micro-tip: To save time, wash, core and slice the apple and cook with 2 tablespoons water at full power for 2 minutes.

WHAT TO DO

1   Pre-heat oven to 180C, 350°F, Gas Mark 4.
2   Place the flour in the mixing bowl and rub in the margarine.
3   Stir in the sugar, add the yoghurt and mix to a soft dough.
4   Knead the dough gently on a floured surface, shape into a 20 cm (8″) circle and lift (carefully) onto the prepared baking tray.
5   Put the base in the oven for 10 minutes.
6   Add the topping: first the banana and raisins, then the stewed apple.
7   Bake for a further 20 minutes.

Eat hot with custard or cold with ice cream . . . and remember to spit out the little green men.

Meet the Crew

BAD GUYS

GOOD GUYS

FIBRE
keeps everyone on
the move

SUGAR
don't let him sweet talk you:
he's no good

VITAMINS & MINERALS
small friends to keep you healthy

ADDITIVES
you're better off without them

PROTEIN
the body builder

FAT
too much will make you greasy and flabby too

CARBOHYDRATES
full of energy

All Aboard....

So it's all aboard the body bus. Into the mouth go the passengers, all jostling for position. Some start misbehaving before they take their seats.

Sugar begins attacking the teeth, while good old fibre, in the form of raw vegetables or crisp fruits, tries to counteract the violence by giving teeth and gums some healthy exercise.

Additives are sly. Some may quietly creep up the back stairs to give you a headache.

A few generous passengers give the body an energy boost straight away. Saliva mixes with the food and carries away some sugar and starch to turn into instant energy.

From the mouth, it's off down the gullet (oesophagus is its other name) into the stomach.

The stomach is a sort of waiting room, where everything we eat awaits its turn to enter the winding, twisting passages of the intestines.

If you eat a lot, quickly, the waiting room gets overfull, you probably know the feeling.

The stomach is a pretty damp place, awash with gastric juices. Every day glands in the bottom of your stomach produce up to six pints of these very acidic juices.

The stomach is something like the antiseptic footbath at the entrance to a swimming pool. One of the functions of these juices is to kill off germs which may have come in on the food.

From the stomach, the food must wait its turn to squeeze through the pyloric sphinctor, which acts like a turnstyle or uniformed commissionaire at the entrance to a football ground or sports centre.

In this case it's the entrance to the intestines (you probably call them guts. It's not a rude word. Even doctors say it.)

If you've had a huge meal it might be quite a struggle keeping the crowds back for the poor old pyloric sphinctor.

You can imagine it shouting: "No pushing at the back, get in line please, only one bun at a time!".

The great voyage of discovery has really begun. First stop is the duodenum, which gets its name from two Latin words meaning 'twelve' (because the duodenum is twelve inches long) and 'hungry'.

Here the food is treated to a good hosing down with powerful digestive juices from the pancreas, and a jet of bile from the gall bladder, which lurks unseen behind the liver.

The rest of the small intestine provides a twisting, turning, rollercoaster ride for our intrepid travellers. They will be tossed about, squeezed and squashed by the muscles along the walls of the eerie tunnel.

Some meals will have a happier ride than others. Those containing plenty of fibre will have a safe, speedy journey. Fibre keeps things moving. It takes on water like a sponge, providing bulk and keeping everyone together, making sure no-one is left behind.

Fibreless meals will have a difficult trip, slow and sluggish. Passengers may fall out of the bus and be left on the roadside for days, until the fibre in a later meal picks up the stragglers.

Diet experts tell us that meals with too little fibre take longer to digest and are more likely to lead to minor blockages in the intestines.

The small intestine is 20 feet long and many of our passengers will not stay on board till the end of the journey, but will disembark to carry out their important work. What we mean is that they are absorbed by the body, and what you eat becomes part of you. You are what you eat!

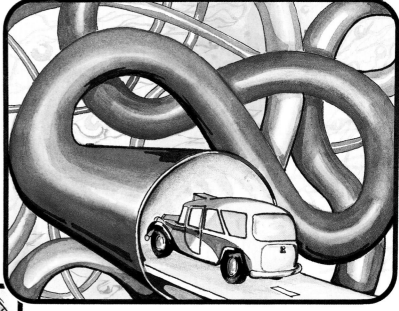

Protein, minerals and vitamins gather up their luggage, wave goodbye to their friends and set off to carry out important construction, repair and maintenance work around the body.

Some calcium stays in the bloodstream to forge a brilliant career in bloodclotting, making nice, crispy scabs when you graze your knees.

Carbohydrates make for the body's power stations, where they are divided into starches and sugars, and set to work giving you energy.

To get to their various workplaces they will leave the body bus and take the advantage of a useful canal system called the bloodstream.

A few lucky nutrients will take a boat trip through one of the two kidneys, which filter the blood, taking out poisons and sending them off down the bladder — a kind of emergency exit. They are flushed out in a liquid called urine. You may have another name for it!

Some workers report to the liver, which is very skilled at sorting and classifying: storing sugar for later use, and making sure foodstuffs don't crowd on to the canal barges and swamp the bloodstream.

The liver also helps the kidneys to filter poisons. This is very important as when the body 'burns' food, the process creates poisons, rather like a car's exhaust.

Bodies that have let too many fats and sugars on board will now experience an overcrowding problem. There's not enough work for all of them, so some are stored as excess flab, piling up on tummies, bottoms and thighs, ganging together to make double chins.

Bodies that have taken large meals with plenty of fibre will fare better. Fibre, like a good driver, stays with the bus all the way to the exit. That's why a jacket potato, huge salad and fresh fruit are less fattening than a few sweets or chips.

Oh no! A fight has broken out! It's those additives again, trying to mug the good guys. Some experts believe that large doses of some chemical additives can destroy some of the nutrients we take such care to include in our meals, or simply stop them being absorbed into the body, so they stay on the bus instead of doing their jobs.

And it's now widely held that some people are actually allergic to some food additives, especially colours.

There are only a few passengers left on the bus by the time it reaches the large intestine, another length of gut, coiled, folded and curved to fit inside the abdomen.

A few workers realise they have missed their stops, rouse themselves, and jump off just in time to join the working parties.

A few waste products stay on the bus till it leaves the body.

And it's now time for the trusty driver, fibre, to unload some of his water supplies.

Water is an important part of the diet. More than half the body's weight is water, and we need to replace the H_2O we lose by sweating and breathing out.

Fibre's next stop is the rectum, where he will prepare to disembark through the exit gate. He keeps a little water with him to help him comfortably out of the door.

People who don't eat enough fibre sometimes find going to the lavatory difficult because their waste matter is too dry and hard. Fibre-eaters never have this problem. Eat as many natural foods as you can and this will never happen to you.

The trip has taken hours to complete, and by the time the last working party has set to work, and the unwanted waste items are on their way to the exit, it's time for the next meal.

Healthy eaters will have found the hunger pangs have not returned for a good few hours after the last mouthful of the last meal was chewed and swallowed.

Those who chose 'junk' food however, may have felt peckish quite soon afterwards. But all that's going to change, isn't it?

Snow Pancakes

Pancakes that melt in your mouth on a winter's day.

You will need

INGREDIENTS

100 g (4 oz) wholewheat flour
1 egg, size 3
150 ml (¼ pt) milk
oil
and a great big handful of clean snow!

EQUIPMENT

mixing bowl
wooden spoon
frying pan
serving plate

WHAT TO DO

1 Put the flour into a mixing bowl and make a well in the middle.
2 Drop the egg and the milk into the well, and beat really hard until it's as smooth as silk.
3 Then, and only then, do you add the magic ingredient — the snow. Mix carefully.
4 Heat a frying pan with a little oil and pour approximately 4 tablespoons of your mixture in. Cook until brown and then turn them over. Ask someone older to toss it just in case you lose your pancake. Repeat until all the mixture is used.

Keep them warm in the oven, and then eat them with a little sugar and lemon juice. Or you might like to eat them with one of these magic fillings:
ice cream, grated chocolate and peanuts, marshmallows, dessicated coconut, stewed apple and cinnamon.

Makes 4–5 pancakes

Apple and Tofu Fluff

You will need

INGREDIENTS

3 large cooking apples, peeled and
stewed with 50 g (2 oz) raw cane sugar
250 g (10 oz) pack silken Tofu
2 eggs, size 4

EQUIPMENT

serving dish
liquidiser
saucepan
dish with 1150 ml (2 pt) capacity

3 mixing bowls, 2 large, 1 small
hand whisk
egg separator
metal spoon

WHAT TO DO

1 Separate the eggs, placing the yolks in the small bowl and the whites in a large one.
2 Beat the yolks into the stewed apple.
3 Drain the liquid from the tofu and liquidise until smooth. Beat into the apple mixture.
4 Using a hand whisk, whisk the egg whites until you can turn the bowl upside down without the mixture moving.
5 Then, using a metal spoon, fold the egg white carefully into the apple mixture.
6 Put in the serving dish and chill thoroughly before serving.

Delicious with wholemeal shortbread.

Pineapple Rafts

Ahoy there! Save a sinking pineapple — send a raft to its rescue. Get your tackle ready. . . .
You will need

INGREDIENTS

4 slices wholemeal bread, spread with vegetable margarine
4 pineapple rings, either fresh or canned in natural juice, drained
2 tablesps. Demerara sugar

EQUIPMENT

bread knife and board
cocktail sticks
baking tray
rice paper
sharp knife
serving plate

WHAT TO DO

1   Pre-heat the oven to 180C, 350°F, Gas Mark 4.
2   Cut each slice of bread into four equal squares.
3   Cut each pineapple ring into four pieces.
4   Put the pieces of bread onto the baking tray and top each with a piece of pineapple.
5   Carefully sprinkle each raft with sugar.
6   Bake for 15–20 minutes, until the bread is crispy and the sugar has turned brown.

Cool slightly before serving, because they will be very hot.
Make sails of rice paper and cocktail sticks beforehand, then launch your rafts on a sea of shredded lettuce.

Polka Dot Rice Pudding

You will need

INGREDIENTS

40 g (1½ oz) short grain brown rice
570 ml (1 pt) skimmed milk
1 ml (¼ teasp.) pure vanilla essence
50 g (2 oz) chocolate chips
150 ml (¼ pt) water
15 ml (1 tablesp.) raw cane sugar

EQUIPMENT

850 ml (1½ pt) ovenproof dish
metal spoon
sieve
measuring jug

WHAT TO DO

1 Pre-heat oven to 170C, 325°F, Gas Mark 3.
2 Wash the short grain rice under running water to remove any dust, etc.
3 Place the 150 ml (¼ pt) water and rice in the ovenproof dish and place on the middle shelf of the oven for 15 minutes. This allows the rice to swell and start to cook. It is important to do this as brown rice requires more liquid to cook in because the husk takes up the increased liquid. Without the extra cooking time the brown rice would be only half cooked making the pudding unpleasant to eat.
4 Remove the dish from the oven. Add the vanilla, sugar, milk and chocolate chips, and then return to the oven for a further hour and a quarter or until the rice is tender.

To serve: eat hot or cold as an ending to any meal.

Open Sesame!

You will need

INGREDIENTS

3 medium cooking apples
30 ml (2 tablesp.) raw cane sugar
25 g (1 oz) large raisins

Crumble
100 g (4 oz) plain wholemeal flour
50 g (2 oz) polyunsaturated margarine
25 g (1 oz) raw cane sugar
25 g (1 oz) sesame seeds

EQUIPMENT

300 ml (½ pt) oven proof dish
sharp knife
saucepan and lid
mixing bowl
metal spoon

WHAT TO DO

1 Wash the apples thoroughly, then cut each apple into four and remove the core.
2 Slice into a saucepan, add the sugar and two tablespoons of water. Simmer until tender — some apples cook quicker than others.
3 Place in the ovenproof dish, add the raisins, then put the dish to one side.
4 Pre-heat oven to 200C, 400°F, Gas Mark 6.
5 Place the flour in a large mixing bowl, rub the margarine into the flour using your fingertips until it resembles fine breadcrumbs.
6 Stir in the sugar and sesame seeds.
7 Sprinkle the crumble evenly over the prepared apple.
8 Bake for 25 minutes until cooked.

Banana Treats

You will need

INGREDIENTS

2 large very ripe bananas
wholemeal self-raising flour
safflower oil for frying

EQUIPMENT

mixing bowl
fork
2 teaspoons
frying pan

2–3 sheets kitchen
paper for draining
draining spoon

METHOD

1 Mash the banana in a mixing bowl and then work in enough flour to give a soft dough.
2 Put enough oil in the frying pan just to cover the bottom and allow to heat through.
3 Using two wetted teaspoons, scoop a heaped teaspoonful of banana mixture and using the second spoon slide it into the heated oil.
4 Turn once during cooking and when cooked drain onto absorbent paper and keep warm in the oven.
5 Repeat until all the mixture has been used up.

Although we are advised not to fry foods, a little occasionally is not going to damage your health. Using safflower oil, which contains very little cholesterol, you will not be eating many saturated fats.

Toasted Rainbow Fruit Salad

You will need

INGREDIENTS

1 red apple
1 green apple
1 banana
1 orange
150 ml (¼ pt) fresh apple juice
Any other *suitable* fruit of your choice:
why not try pears, grapes, plums, fresh
peaches. . . .

Toasted Topping
45 ml (3 tablesps.) desiccated coconut
15 ml (1 tablesp.) sunflower seeds
25 g (1 oz) chopped nuts — e.g. peanuts,
almonds
500 ml (1–2 pt) serving dish

EQUIPMENT

sharp knife
chopping board
serving plate
ovenproof plate

WHAT TO DO

1   Prepare the fruit by washing first and leaving on any edible skins so as to increase
the fibre content of the dish. Cut, using a sharp vegetable knife, into *bite size* pieces.
Place these into the serving bowl along with the fresh apple juice.

2   *The topping*: place all 3 ingredients on to the plate and toast under the grill — until
they are a golden brown colour.

3   Whilst still warm sprinkle over the prepared fruit. Serve at once.

Serve with Fromage Frais or natural yoghurt.

Makes 4–6 portions

Summer Flan

You will need

INGREDIENTS

Flan base
2 eggs, size 2
50 g (2 oz) Golden Granulated sugar
50 g (2 oz) wholemeal flour
5 ml (1 heaped teasp.) rice flour

Filling
fresh summer fruits, e.g. peaches,
strawberries, raspberries
Glaze
15 ml (1 heaped tablesp.) arrowroot
10 ml (1 dessertsp.) clear honey
200 ml (⅓ pint) water

EQUIPMENT

mixing bowl
metal spoon
wire rack
electric mixer (or hand whisk)
spatula

WHAT TO DO

1 Pre-heat the oven to 220C, 425°F, Gas Mark 7.

2 Prepare the flan tin. I always grease if using a non-stick tin, but grease and line the base of an ordinary tin.

3 *Prepare the flan.*
(i) Whisk the eggs and sugar until the mixture is thick and creamy or until you can leave a trail of the figure 8 on the surface for a count of 4.
(ii) Mix the two flours together thoroughly and then very gently fold in the flour mixture using a metal spoon, making a figure of eight movement and taking care not to miss any of the flour which may settle at the bottom of the bowl.
(iii) Pour sponge mixture into prepared tin, holding bowl near tin so as not to knock out any of the air.
(iv) Bake for 12 minutes until well risen.
(v) Allow to cool for a few minutes in the tin, then turn out onto the rack to cool. When cold, fill with fruit.

4 Make the arrowroot glaze.
(i) Mix all the ingredients together.
(ii) Bring to the boil slowly, stirring all the time until clear and thick.
(iii) Stir until slightly cooled and then pour over the fruit, making sure that it is all coated. This will keep it moist.

Eat on the same day.
Serves 4–6

Thatched Marmalade Cake

You will need

INGREDIENTS

100 g (4 oz) polyunsaturated margarine
100 g (4 oz) caster sugar
2 eggs, size 4
125 g (5 oz) self-raising wholemeal flour
15 ml (6 level tablesps.) reduced sugar marmalade
2 thick slices wholemeal bread with the crusts cut off.

EQUIPMENT

mixing bowl
wooden spoon
metal spoon
bread knife
sieve
8″ tall cake tin — lined with greaseproof paper — like the one you make a Christmas cake in.

WHAT TO DO

1 Pre-heat the oven to 200C, 400°F, Gas Mark 6.

2 Cream the fat and sugar together until pale in colour.

3 Beat the eggs in a separate bowl using a fork.

4 Gradually add the egg to the mixture — beat well.

5 Sieve flour and fold into the mixture using a large metal spoon.

6 Have ready the lined tin, the prepared cake mixture, and the marmalade, and the bread cut roughly into cubes.

7 Firstly place half the cake mixture in the cake tin, then simply drop the six tablespoons of marmalade on to the cake mixture, and pile on the remaining cake mixture.

8 To add the thatching — place the cubes of bread at random over the surface of the cake.

9 Bake for 1 hour.

Allow to cool in the tin. This cake is better if it is left and eaten the next day.

Makes 6–8 portions

Carob Digestives

You will need

INGREDIENTS

50–75 g (2–3 oz) dates
50 g (2 oz) unsalted peanuts
10 ml (2 teasps.) aniseed
10 ml (2 teasps.) sesame seed
100 ml (4 fl. oz) olive oil or sunflower oil
rind and juice of one orange
200 g (8 oz) wholemeal flour

5 ml (1 teasps.) cinnamon
15 ml (3 teasps.) carob powder
1 small egg

For the topping
1 egg white
25 g (1 oz) finely chopped peanuts

EQUIPMENT

small saucepan
fork
liquidiser
baking tray
5 cm (2") cutter
rolling pin
flour dredger
mixing bowl

WHAT TO DO

1 Pre-heat oven to 180C, 350°F, Gas Mark 4.
2 Cook dates gently in a little water until soft, drain and beat to a stiff purée with a fork.
3 Grind the peanuts, aniseed and sesame seeds, and place in a large bowl.
4 Slowly mix in the oil, then add the orange rind and juice, and puréed dates.
5 Add the flour, cinnamon and carob powder. Stir again.
6 Beat in the egg and mix to a stiff dough.
7 Turn onto a floured work surface. Roll out and cut into biscuit shapes, or divide the mixture into walnut sized pieces and press into individual rounds.
8 Brush with egg white and scatter with peanuts.
9 Bake on a greased tray for 25–30 minutes.

Chinese Fortune Cookies

You will need

INGREDIENTS

250 g (8 oz) brown sugar eg Golden
Granulated sugar
100 g (4 oz) butter
50 g (2 oz) oats
50 g (2 oz) ground almonds

25 g (1 oz) flaked almonds
25 g (1 oz) coconut
few drops almond essence
75 g (3 oz) wholemeal flour
18–20 fortunes on little pieces of paper

EQUIPMENT

mixing bowl
round-ended knife
wooden spoon
greased baking sheet

flour dredger
cooking rack
small bowl

WHAT TO DO

1   Pre-heat oven to 170C, 325°F, Gas Mark 3.
2   Cream the fat and sugar together.
3   Put the oats, almonds, almond essence and coconut in a bowl and stir.
4   Mix in a spoonful of the oat mixture and the flour alternatively mixing well between additions, until the mixture is stiff to handle. Dust your hands with a little flour and roll into balls the size of a walnut. At this point pop your little piece of paper into the biscuits, seal well.
5   Place on a lightly greased baking tray with enough room to spread. There will be about 8 biscuits per tray.
6   Bake for 20–25 minutes until slightly risen, and golden brown on the bottom.

Allow to cool and then break in half to see what your good fortune for the rest of the day will be.

Makes 18–20 biscuits

Knave of Hearts Tart

The Queen of Hearts   She made some tarts,   All on a summer's day.

You will need

INGREDIENTS

Pastry Case
100 g (4 oz) fine milled plain wholemeal flour
50 g (2 oz) polyunsaturated margarine
enough ice-cold water to make a firm dough

Filling (All-in-one sponge mixture)
50 g (2 oz) polyunsaturated margarine
50 g (2 oz) soft brown sugar
1 egg, size 3/4
50 g (2 oz) self-raising wholemeal flour
25 g (1 oz) flaked almonds
30 ml (2 tablesps.) sugar-free raspberry jam

EQUIPMENT

mixing bowl
round-ended knife
rolling pin
fluted flan ring
wooden spoon

WHAT TO DO

1   Pre-heat the oven to 180C, 350°F, Gas Mark 4.

2   *Make the pastry*: rubbing the fat into the flour until it resembles breadcrumbs, and add enough ice-cold water to make a firm dough.

3   Knead gently on a floured surface until smooth, roll out to fit and line a fluted flan dish. Spread the raspberry jam over the base and put in the fridge.

4   *Prepare the filling*: place the margarine and sugar in a mixing bowl and beat until light and fluffy. Add the eggs and flour and mix well. Spread evenly over the base. Sprinkle the flaked almonds over the surface.

5   Bake for 40–45 minutes. until risen and golden brown.

Delicious eaten hot or cold.
If you would prefer individual bakewells, line a 12-spaced pattie tin with the pastry, a dab of jam and a heaped spoonful of sponge mixture and sprinkle with almonds. Bake for 30 minutes.

Sticky Fingers

A Bran Loaf

Use your loaf when following this recipe. Use a teacup as a measure — and remember it must be the same one throughout, not cups of different sizes, or the results could be very strange.

You will need

INGREDIENTS

1 cup mixed dried fruit
1 cup soya milk
1 cup raw cane sugar
1 cup bran
1 cup wholemeal flour

EQUIPMENT

cup
flat-bottomed loaf tin
mixing bowl
metal spoon
aluminium foil

WHAT TO DO

1 Grease a deep-based loaf tin.
2 Mix the dried fruit and soya milk in a bowl and leave for at least 10 minutes.
3 Pre-heat the oven to 180C, 350°F, Gas Mark 4.
4 Add all the other ingredients to the fruit mixture and mix well.
5 Put the mixture in the prepared tin.
6 Bake until firm to the touch (test with a skewer after 35 minutes).
7 To make it sticky, wrap the loaf in aluminium foil while hot and leave until the next day.

To serve: slice and add the spread of your choice.

Makes 8–10 slices

Victoria Sponge Cake

You will need

INGREDIENTS

100 g (4 oz) polyunsaturated margarine
100 g (4 oz) raw cane sugar
2 eggs, size 3/4
100 g (4 oz) self-raising wholemeal flour

2 tablesps. boiling water
sugar reduced jam or spread for the filling

EQUIPMENT

mixing bowl
wooden spoon
metal spoon
2 sandwich tins
wire rack

small bowl
fork
sieve
greaseproof paper

WHAT TO DO

1 Pre-heat the oven to 180C, 350°F, Gas Mark 4.
2 *Prepare sandwich tins*: lightly grease and line base with greaseproof paper.
3 Cream the fat and sugar with the wooden spoon until it is pale in colour.
4 Beat the eggs in a separate bowl and add to the creamed mixture, beating well.
5 Change from a wooden spoon to a metal spoon, and fold in the sieved wholemeal flour, adding it a little at a time.
6 Divide evenly between prepared sandwich tins.
7 Bake for 20–25 minutes until well risen and brown. Cool on a wire rack.
8 When cold, sandwich together using the filling of your choice.

This freezes well so you could make two at a time to use for unexpected guests.

Honey Biscuits

You will need

INGREDIENTS

90 ml (6 tablesps.) sunflower oil
50 g (2 oz) polyunsaturated margarine
90 ml (6 tablesps.) honey
300 g (10 oz) wholemeal plain flour

5 ml (1 teasp.) baking powder
30 ml (2 tablesps.) wheatgerm
pinch of all-spice

EQUIPMENT

mixing bowl
teaspoon
cooling rack
wooden spoon
2–3 baking trays

WHAT TO DO

1   Pre-heat the oven to 190C, 375°F, Gas Mark 5.
2   Put the oil, margarine and honey into a mixing bowl and stir but do not beat.
3   Work in all other ingredients, using the wooden spoon, until well mixed.
4   Using a wetted teaspoon drop spoonfuls of mixture onto a greased baking tray.
    Allow space for them to spread.
5   Bake for 12–15 minutes. until brown underneath.
6   Cool on a wire rack.

Makes 30 biscuits

Sunset Cake

Yes, it really has got carrots in it — and oranges for sunshine.

You will need

INGREDIENTS

125 g (4 oz) polyunsaturated margarine
125 g (4 oz) raw cane sugar
2 eggs, size 2
250 g (8 oz) plain wholemeal flour
125 g (4 oz) raisins

5 ml (1 teasp.) baking powder
250 g (8 oz) grated carrot
juice and rind of one orange
125 g (4 oz) chopped nuts (e.g. almonds, hazelnuts)

EQUIPMENT

mixing bowl
wooden spoon
scales
chopping board

23 cm (9″) cake tin, greased and lined
knife
grater

WHAT TO DO

1   Pre-heat the oven to 180C, 350°F, Gas Mark 4.

2   Cream the fat and sugar.

3   Add all the other ingredients and beat well with a wooden spoon or spatula until thoroughly mixed.

4   Turn mixture into the greased and lined cake tin.

5   Bake for 45–55 minutes, until firm to the touch. Allow to cool in the tin.

Pussy-Cat Pizza

Before you start chasing the family cat around the house, I have to tell you that there are NO cats in this recipe.
You will need

INGREDIENTS

200 g (8 oz) self-raising wholemeal flour
50 g (2 oz) polyunsaturated margarine
150 ml (¼ pt) natural yoghurt

For the Topping
1 can tomatoes, chopped
100 g (4 oz) grated cheese

For the Face
2 olives — for the eyes
strips of pepper — for the nose and whiskers

EQUIPMENT

mixing bowl
round-ended knife
rolling pin

greased baking tray
sharp knife
grater

WHAT TO DO

1 Pre-heat oven to 220C, 425°F, Gas Mark 7.
2 Place the flour into a large mixing bowl and rub in the margarine, until it looks like fine breadcrumbs.
3 Mix to a soft dough with the yoghurt.
4 Place on a floured surface and knead until smooth.
5 Roll out to a circle. Using a sharp knife cut out the following shape:
6 Transfer to a baking tray greased with vegetable oil.
7 Spread the chopped tomato over the base, then the grated cheese, and finally make the face using the olives and pepper.
8 Bake for 35 minutes until golden brown.

Serve hot or cold with salad or coleslaw.
Your Pussy-Cat Pizza tastes purr-fect don't you agree?

Bonfire Soup

You will need

INGREDIENTS

30 ml (2 tablesps.) sunflower oil or corn oil
1 onion, peeled, chopped
2 carrots, sliced
3 sticks celery, sliced
1 small green pepper, deseeded, diced
50 g (2 oz) long grain brown rice
30 ml (2 tablesps.) Pesto (basil sauce) — (optional)
1 clove garlic, crushed (optional)

1 large tin tomatoes, chopped
15 ml (1 tablesp.) tomato purée
600 ml (1 pt) water or stock
30 ml (2 tablesps.) chopped fresh parsley

Pesto (basil sauce) is a combination of the herb basil, oil, cheese, pine kernals, and carobseed powder, and finally a pinch of salt. It is used in Italian cooking and adds a final touch to many dishes.

EQUIPMENT

large saucepan with lid
sharp knife
chopping board
mugs to serve
measuring jug

WHAT TO DO

1   Heat oil, add the chopped onion, cook slowly for 2–3 minutes. Then add the crushed garlic. Cook for 2 minutes.
2   Add the carrots and celery, and cook for a further 5 minutes.
3   Then add the green pepper, tinned tomatoes, tomato purée, the stock or water, and the washed brown rice.
4   Simmer slowly for 35 minutes or until the rice is cooked.
5   Before serving, add the chopped parsley and Pesto. Serve in mugs.

Fruitie Bonfire Punch

You will need

INGREDIENTS

20 ml (4 tablesps.) blackcurrant cordial
juice and rind of an orange and lemon
4 tablesps. sugar — raw cane
1.1 litres (2 pts.) water
1 apple

EQUIPMENT

large saucepan
wooden spoon
lemon squeezer
sharp knife
measuring jug

WHAT TO DO

1　Put the water in a large saucepan and heat.
2　Stir in the sugar, lemon and orange juice, using a wooden spoon.
3　Bring to the boil, then switch off.
4　Add the blackcurrant cordial.
5　Pour into a punch bowl and slice the apple, and float the fruit.

Delicious and warming for a cold Bonfire night party.

Serves 6

Chick Pea Pasties

You will need

INGREDIENTS

Pastry
150 g (6 oz) wholemeal flour
75 g (3 oz) polyunsaturated margarine
enough cold water to make a soft dough

Filling
1 tablesp. sunflower oil
1 small onion, diced
75 g (3 oz) mushrooms, wiped and diced

75 g (3 oz) potatoes, scrubbed and diced
good pinch mixed herbs
3 ml (½ teasp.) marmite
50 g (2 oz) chick peas — soaked overnight
and cooked for 20 minutes in plenty of
water, drained.

Glaze
a little beaten egg or milk

EQUIPMENT

mixing bowl
rolling pin
frying pan

WHAT TO DO

1   Pre-heat oven to 200C, 400°F, Gas Mark 6.
2   Prepare the pastry by rubbing in the margarine until it resembles breadcrumbs.
3   Make to a soft dough using the cold water. Put in the fridge to relax whilst you prepare the filling.
4   To make the filling: heat oil in the frying pan, add the onion, fry for 2 minutes and then add all the other ingredients and gently fry for a further 10 minutes.
    Micro-tip: combine all ingredients, cover and microwave on full power for 10 mins. Stir regularly. Allow to cool and mix in the cooked chick peas.
4   Divide the pastry into 4 equal pieces and roll each into a circle. Divide the mixture between them. Add a sprinkling of black pepper, then fold over and seal the edges using a little water.
5   Brush with egg and place on a baking tray. Bake for 15–20 minutes.

Grasmere Gingerbread

You will need

INGREDIENTS

200 g (8 oz) wholemeal self-raising flour
100 g (4 oz) moist muscavado sugar
100 g (4 oz) polyunsaturated margarine
10 ml (2 teasps.) ground ginger
50 g (2 oz) chopped peel

EQUIPMENT

mixing bowl
175 mm (7″) sandwich tin or flan ring—
metal preferably
tablespoon

WHAT TO DO

1 Pre-heat oven to 180C, 350°F, Gas Mark 4.

2 Place the flour in a mixing bowl. Rub in the margarine.

3 Stir in the sugar, ginger and mixed peel, reserving 2 tablespoons to use as topping.

4 Continue kneading until you have formed a ball of dough.

5 Press into the greased baking tin/metal flan ring.

6 Bake for 35 minutes. Remove and sprinkle over the topping and return to the oven for a further 15 minutes or until firm to the touch.

Allow to cool in the tin and then cut into portions.

Makes 4 generous portions

Christmas Tree Special

You will need

INGREDIENTS

200 g (7 oz) wholemeal flour
25 g (1 oz) corn flour
100 g (4 oz) polyunsaturated margarine
— chill well
enough ice cold water to make a soft
dough

Filling
6 tablespoons cooked mincemeat
5 colour free glacé cherries

EQUIPMENT

sharp knife
ruler
baking tray
rolling pin
pastry brush

WHAT TO DO

1 Pre-heat oven to 180C, 350°F, Gas Mark 4.

2 *Prepare the pastry*: mix the two flours together in a large mixing bowl. Rub in the fat and mix to a soft dough using the ice cold water.

3 Knead gently to remove any cracks and roughly shape into a rectangle.

4 Roll out the rectangle until it measures 30 cm x 18 cm (12 x 7″).

5 Using a sharp knife cut out the following Christmas Tree shape. If you find this a little difficult draw a template on paper, cut it out and cut around it. Keep the template to cut around the next time you want to make it.

6 With the remaining pastry cut 1 cm (½″) strips, dampen the edge with a wet pastry brush and place over the edge to make a border to look like this:
Place on a greased baking tray and bake until golden brown (about 15 minutes). Transfer to a flat serving plate.

7 Fill the middle with mincemeat and place the cherries on the tips of the branches.

It looks splendid as a centre piece for Christmas — you can warm it through if you prefer — and it tastes delicious with thick set natural yoghurt.

Summertime Sundaes

You will need

INGREDIENTS

2 carob digestives, crushed
1 pot strawberry Fromage Frais
30 ml (2 tablesps.) clear honey
50 g (2 oz) carob chips
60 ml (4 tablesps.) dried banana chips

1 punnet strawberries (keep 2 large ones for the top)
1 small carton Quark *or* thick set sheeps yoghurt

EQUIPMENT

2 sundae glasses
2 long spoons
chopping board
sieve

tablespoon
plastic bag
& rolling pin
sharp knife

WHAT TO DO

This takes quite some time to do, so get everything ready first.

1   Crush the biscuits in the plastic bag, using the rolling pin. Put into glasses and dribble honey on top.

2   Chop strawberries. Put a little chopped strawberry into each glass.

3   Layer with some Fromage Frais, then carob chips and some more Fromage Frais.

4   Crush banana chips, divide between glasses, then fill each glass with more chopped strawberry until it comes above the top of the glass.

5   Finally put the most enormous dollop of Quark or thick set yoghurt on top and crown with the reserved strawberries.

Makes 2 sundaes

Spicy Chick Pea Nibbles

You will need

INGREDIENTS

225 g (8 oz) chick peas
15–30 ml (1–2 tablesps.) curry powder
(mild or hot)
30 ml (2 tablesps.) corn oil

EQUIPMENT

large saucepan and lid
roasting tin

WHAT TO DO

You have to start this the day before, by soaking the chick peas in a large bowl of water overnight.

1   Put the soaked chick peas into a large saucepan and fill the saucepan with cold water.

2   Put on to boil, cover and boil until chick peas are tender, for 40–50 minutes. Add more water if necessary.

3   Drain the chick peas and put to one side.

4   While the chick peas are cooking, pre-heat oven to 140C, 275°F, Gas Mark 1. Take a roasting tin and put on the oil, heat in the oven, and then sprinkle on the curry powder and mix with oil.

5   Add the chick peas, mix and return to the oven for 20 minutes.

To serve: sprinkle with a little salt and eat hot or cold.

Apricot Whipped Flan

You will need

INGREDIENTS

Base
125 g (5 oz) additive-free digestive biscuits
30–45 ml (2–3 tablesps.) soya oil

Decoration
angelica

Filling
175 g (6 oz) dried apricots, soaked overnight
225 g (8 oz) natural Fromage Frais
30 ml (2 tablesps.) clear honey

EQUIPMENT

13 cm (7″) flan dish (pottery)
wooden spoon
small saucepan
rolling pin
medium mixing bowl
plastic bag
metal tablespoon

WHAT TO DO

1 Place the biscuits in the plastic bag and reduce to crumbs by rolling them with the rolling pin.

2 Place the oil in the saucepan and warm gently. Pour in the crumbs and mix well. Line the base and sides of the flan dish with crumb mixture. Pop in the fridge to firm up.

3 Meanwhile, wash the saucepan and cook the apricots in 275 ml (½ pt) cold water, until tender and nearly all the liquid has disappeared. Remove 4 well shaped apricots to use as decoration.

4 Beat the apricots in the bowl with the wooden spoon to make an even consistency. Then using the metal spoon fold in the honey and Fromage Frais until all ingredients are well mixed.

5 Spread this mixture over the biscuit base and decorate with reserved apricots and angelica.

Serves 4

Crunchy Apple Ice Cream

You will need

INGREDIENTS

150 ml (¼ pt) skimmed milk
100 g (4 oz) polyunsaturated margarine
5 ml (1 teasp.) gelatine
175 g (6 oz) Apple and Raisin Crunchy

Breakfast Cereal (unsweetened)
2 egg whites, size 1
200 g (8 oz) raw cane sugar
150 ml (¼ pt) water

EQUIPMENT

liquidiser
milk pan
hand whisk
tablespoon

plastic freezer dish
wooden spoon
2 mixing bowls

WHAT TO DO

Stage 1

1 Heat the milk and margarine and gelatine until melted. Stir well using the wooden spoon.

2 Pour into the liquidiser and blend for 2 minutes. Pour into a bowl and put to one side.

Stage 2

1 Bring the water and sugar to the boil and then simmer gently for 5 minutes until the syrup is formed.

2 In a clean mixing bowl whisk the egg whites until stiff. Keep beating until the mixture forms firm peaks and the bowl can be turned upside down without spilling.

3 Continue beating whilst adding the hot syrup in a steady stream. You will probably need help with this.

4 Beat until thick and stiff. Leave to stand for 5 minutes. Rebeat until cool.

5 Using a metal spoon fold in the milk mixture and the Apple and Raisin Breakfast Cereal.

6 Turn into the plastic dish and place in a freezer. Freeze until solid.

For best results use a freezer as this reaches a temperature of below 20°C, whereas a domestic freezer compartment in a fridge only keeps pre-frozen items frozen.

Serves 4–6 portions

Melting Moments

(Almond Ring)

You will need

INGREDIENTS

Base
100 g (4 oz) raw cane sugar
75 g (3 oz) wholemeal flour
25 g (1 oz) brown rice flour
100 g (4 oz) polyunsaturated margarine
1 egg yolk, size 2

Topping
1 egg white, size 2
100 g (4 oz) ground almonds
sugar-free raspberry jam

EQUIPMENT

mixing bowl
wooden spoon
hand whisk
palette knife
baking tray
rolling pin
flour dredger
wire cooling rack

WHAT TO DO

1 Pre-heat the oven to 190C, 375°F, Gas Mark 5.
2 Cream the fat and sugar together.
3 Beat in the egg yolk and then work in the flour.
4 Form into a ball and roll out to a 20 cm (8") circle. Place on a baking tray.
5 Spread with sugar-free jam.
6 Wash and carefully dry the bowl and whisk the egg white until it stands in peaks by itself. Then fold in the ground almonds, using metal spoon.
7 Spread evenly over the base.
8 Bake for 25–35 minutes until golden. Cool on wire rack.
9 Cut into wedges. It is quite sweet, so only have on special occasions.

Makes 1 ring

Pop Corn

You will need

INGREDIENTS

50 g (2 oz) popping corn
15 ml (1 tablesp.) soya oil

EQUIPMENT

heavy saucepan with a well fitting lid
draining spoon
serving bowl

WHAT TO DO

1 Place the oil in the saucepan and put on a moderate heat with the lid on. Heat for 1 minute.
2 Add the corn to the saucepan and quickly replace the lid. Lower the heat.
3 The next thing to happen will be loud popping noises as the nibblets of corn split and turn themselves inside out. When all the popping has finished, have a look in the saucepan, and there you will find a whole saucepan full of delicious popped corn. You can eat it whilst it's still warm or you can use one of the following ingredients to stir in to make your popcorn extra special:

20 ml (2 dessertsps.) clear honey and 25 g (1 oz) chopped nuts
20 ml (1 heaped tablesp.) Pear and Apple spread
5 ml (1 teasp.) curry powder
15 ml (1 tablesp.) maple syrup

Cheese Straws

You will need

INGREDIENTS

200 g (8 oz) wholemeal flour
100 g (4 oz) polyunsaturated margarine
75 g (3 oz) fat reduced cheddar cheese
good pinch cayenne pepper
1 egg yolk, size 2
10 ml (2 teasps.) cold water

EQUIPMENT

mixing bowl
round-ended knife
grater
egg separator
baking tray

sharp knife
selection of small cutters
rolling pin
wire rack

WHAT TO DO

1   Pre-heat the oven to 180C, 350°F, Gas Mark 4.

2   Place the flour in the mixing bowl and rub in the margarine.

3   Finely grate the cheese and stir into the mixture.

4   Add the cayenne pepper.

5   Mix to a soft dough using the egg yolk and cold water. Knead gently until smooth.

6   Roll out on a floured surface to 6 cm (¼") thickness.

7   Using a sharp knife (and a ruler if you do not have a steady hand) cut 6 cm (¼") strips and transfer to a baking tray that has been floured rather than greased. This is to absorb the fat from the cheese which melts during cooking.
    If you prefer you can use a selection of small cutters to add variety to your biscuits.

8   Bake for 5–6 minutes only, watching carefully as they burn easily. Cool on a wire rack. Keep in an airtight tin.

Makes enough to serve 4–6

Real Fruit Milk Shakes

You will need

INGREDIENTS

275 ml (½ pt) well chilled skimmed milk and 40 ml (2 heaped tablesp.) powdered skimmed milk. Try *one* of the following to make a really delicious milk shake.
6 strawberries,
1 mashed banana,
5 ml (1 teasp.) carob powder and
5 ml (1 teasp.) ground almonds,

12 raspberries,
10 ml (2 teasp.) clear honey and
3 ml (½ teasp.) pure vanilla,
15 ml (1 tablesp.) desiccated coconut and 1 slice pineapple

EQUIPMENT

liquidiser
teaspoon
tablespoon
fork (to mash banana)
tall glass

WHAT TO DO

1 Place the milk and milk powder in the liquidiser, put lid on firmly and blend until smooth.

2 Add the flavouring of your choice. Blend again and pour out into a tall glass.

Almond and Honey Night Cap

You will need

INGREDIENTS

575 ml (1 pt) skimmed milk
20 ml (2 heaped dessertsps.) ground
almonds
6 ml (2 teasps.) clear honey

EQUIPMENT

milk pan
dessertspoon
teaspoon
2 half pint mugs

WHAT TO DO

1   Heat the milk in the saucepan until just boiling. Put the milk in the mugs.
2   Stir in 1 teaspoon honey to each mug and then sprinkle the ground almonds on the
    top. Allow to stand for 30 seconds before drinking so as to let the flavours mingle.

This is very relaxing on a cold winter's evening.

Makes 2 mugs

Pink Whiskers Drink

It's frothy, it's fruity and it's fun! Want to know why it's called Pink Whiskers Drink?
Well, take a sip and go and look in the mirror. That's why!

You will need

INGREDIENTS

300 ml (½ pt) natural yoghurt
150 ml (¼ pt) skimmed milk
150 ml (¼ pt) fizzy mineral water

a large assortment of fruit, e.g. raspberries, peaches, strawberries, bananas, plums

EQUIPMENT

liquidiser
measuring jug
2 tall glasses

WHAT TO DO

1 Place the yoghurt and skimmed milk in the liquidiser for 30 seconds.
2 Add the fruits of your choice and liquidise for a further 30 seconds.
3 Pour into tall glasses until two thirds full and top up with fizzy mineral water.

Why not decorate the glasses with cherries and orange and lemon slices on cocktail
sticks to make your drinks look even more attractive?
Very refreshing on hot days.